THE
DIVINE

BY
DAWN WARMACK

Library of Congress Control Number:

2024915936

Published by Hemingway Publishers

Cover design by Hemingway Publishers

ISBN: Printed in the United States

Dedication

In dedication to my Grandmother Hazel, who is such a huge part of who I am today.

I also dedicate this book to my son Andrew, my family, and anyone who has inspired me throughout the years.

Acknowledgment

I would like to acknowledge the Hemingway Publishing Company for the Publishing of this book.

Table of Contents

About the Author

Dawn Warmack is an American Author. Born in a small town in Michigan, she believes in following your dreams and that with trusting in faith, anything is possible. That *Love* is the most powerful source in all things.

Chapter 1
1888 Boston, Massachusetts

The Stories Unveil

It was 1888 in Boston, Massachusetts. The night descended upon the city like a heavy shroud, cloaking the streets in an eerie silence broken only by the distant rumble of thunder. Dark clouds loomed overhead with the promise of a storm. The air was thick with the scent of rain and something more sinister, a foreboding sense of unease that hung over the city like a curse.

In the heart of this gloom, tales drifted like whispers on the Wind, and stories sailed across the sea with many travelers seeking escape from the darkness that surrounded Whitechapel, London. Many feared the plaque of death that seemed to linger in the air, a specter that haunted the very streets of Massachusetts as visitors arrived.

Rumors swirled throughout the night, whispered in hushed tones behind closed doors. A murderer was said to be on the loose, and his identity was unknown. With at least eleven unsolved murders haunting the streets and countless others missing, the name "Jack the Ripper" echoed throughout the city, shaking the walls and instilling fear in the hearts of the citizens of Massachusetts. The fear continued as newcomers would disembark the ships to tell stories of this haunting tragedy.

xxx

I, Cora Hughes, was intrigued by this "Jack the Ripper". The thought of a murderer stalking the streets, preying on the innocent, sent a chill down my spine, but even with the crippling fear, my head was filled with unanswered questions. *Who is he? Did he really murder all these people? Why are all the murders unsolved?*

And most importantly, why do I care? As I lay in my bed, listening to the distant rumble of thunder, I couldn't shake the feeling of unease that gripped me. The darkness seemed to press in from all sides, suffocating my every thought.

I tossed and turned, unable to find peace, my mind consumed by this murderer on the loose. And with a huge sigh, all the pondering thoughts collapsed altogether.

What was I doing here? Is this really what I wanted to do with my life? To grow old with no story to tell? In that moment, a spark of curiosity flickered to life within me.

I always wanted to travel and wondered where my life would be if I left Massachusetts. I knew that what I wanted to do was far greater than living day to day in this small, forgotten town. I had so much more to offer this world. I had always been drawn to mysteries, to the secrets that lay hidden beneath the surface. The idea of uncovering the truth behind the terror of Jack the Ripper filled me with a sense of purpose; I wanted to unveil the truth, to peel back the layers of fear and mystery enveloping Whitechapel. This was more than a mere fascination; it was a calling.

I had a plan on how to get out, but it was going to take some work on my end. I pulled out my journal and began to write, the ink flowing like a river of hope across the pages. Trying to put down in detail what I wanted and how I needed to get it. It seemed like hours went by just sitting in my bedroom, the candle burning low as my thoughts raced ahead of my pen.

I found myself daydreaming about different outcomes and how my family might react to such a huge change if I left Massachusetts. Then I thought, why tell my family? It would only make matters worse if they knew what I was planning. They definitely wouldn't agree or let me go. But I knew I had to do something to help these people in Whitechapel. After all, investigating was something I enjoyed, a passion that thrived in the shadows of this small town. You could pretty much have a field day with all the married couples engaging in extramarital affairs and finding out who stole something from the general store. The town was buried with thousands of secrets, surrounded by the darkness waiting to be unraveled.

I don't think most people really cared about looking into it. Most just tried to avoid confrontation and act as if it didn't exist. They were shielding themselves from the very existence of this messy reality. On the other hand, I preferred to do research and see what was really going on. I was more of the silent type, a dreamer at heart, always trying to find something out but never telling anyone. Besides, who would believe me anyways?

And honestly, no one I knew of except my grandmother. She passed away about five years ago. She said I reminded her of herself when she was younger. I didn't think that was a bad thing. She was the sweetest person you could ever meet, her kindness lighting my path like the North Star in a stormy sky. The only thing I have to remember her by is this cross necklace she gave me. As she lay in bed, taking her last breath, she pressed the necklace into my hand, her voice a fragile whisper. She told me this necklace would protect me from evil forces.

"You are different," She murmured, her voice like a gentle wind stirring the still air. "And when the time comes, you will understand what I mean." She started rambling on about special powers and insight I would receive during this time. I had no clue what she was talking about. To be completely honest, my mind was a whirlwind of sadness and confusion, and I couldn't think much about the words she uttered as I was watching her take her last breath.

"Don't worry, Grandma, one day I'll make you proud," I remembered saying to myself as she slowly drifted off.

The storm outside mirrored the thunder within me. Lightning flashed, illuminating the room for a brief second in quick, bright flashes, and thunder boomed like a giant drum. My eyes diverted from my journal towards the open window; to me, it felt like nature was as determined as I was. And I was ready to leave behind the safety of the known for the perils of the unknown.

I finally had the chance to show her. Even though she wasn't here, she was with me in spirit. This was my chance to get out of this obliterated town and do something that made a difference. Something that no one would expect. I couldn't waste my life away anymore. I had to get out. It was now or never.

Chapter 2
Leaving Massachusetts

I decided to close my eyes, and I drifted off to sleep, eager for the journey that lie ahead. A journey I knew would change my life forever. My heart was a drum, pounding with excitement at the thought of what was to come. I had to prepare meticulously, ensuring I had everything I might need. My mind raced as I wrote down my list: writing utensils, my journal, food, and clothes, and the list seemed endless, but one destination was clear: Whitechapel, London. The very name sent a shiver down my spine. It was as if the mere mention of it whispered secrets of shadows and danger. This was the most dangerous city I had ever gone to. My heart pounded in my chest, a wild drumbeat echoing my fear and excitement. Images of the dark, fog-laden streets filled my mind, where every corner seemed to hide a lurking menace. Stories of Jack the Ripper's terror gripped my imagination, his shadowy figure haunting my thoughts.

I decided to grab a few protective items to take with me. It couldn't hurt - better to be safe than sorry. My hands trembled as I packed, the reality of my choice sinking in with each item I placed in my bag, yet something in me had me enthralled. I had a few knives and an Enfield Revolver my grandfather gave me. I imagined him beside me, his stern yet loving presence guiding me through the darkness. I can't imagine not taking this with me, I thought. As much as I was afraid, I knew I may need this where I was headed. I tried to be discreet when packing it. I can't imagine they'd let me on a ship knowing I was carrying these things.

As the sun set and the shadows lengthened, I stood by the window, staring out into the gathering night. The streets outside seemed to blur, merging with the dark alleys of Whitechapel in my mind. A chill ran through me, but within that fear was a tiny ember of courage that refused to be extinguished.

My thoughts rumbled, and my mind was racing. Going alone wasn't on my list. Obviously, I didn't want to go alone. *But who would be that crazy,* I thought. I needed maybe Charlie, the neighbor down the road. He never liked living here. I don't know. I needed to stay focused. But then, I remembered Henry. He would go with me. He had just lost his wife and was completely alone. It couldn't hurt to ask. Perhaps I would just tell him we were going to Greenwich, London. He wouldn't suspect a thing, especially since I had family members that lived there.

I decided to go back to sleep for a few hours. My mind was a whirlwind of thoughts and I knew I needed the rest. According to what I heard, a ship was heading out in the morning, and I wanted to be on it. I double-checked my bags, ensuring everything was in order.

As morning approached, I jumped out of bed, grabbed my things, and headed for the door. The early dawn light streamed through the window, casting a golden hue across the room. The silence of the house was almost deafening, broken only by the distant chirping of birds waking to a new day. My heart pounded with a mix of excitement and anxiety as I mentally checked off my list once more. But just as I reached for the doorknob, a sudden realization struck me like a bolt of lightning – I was missing the cross necklace my grandmother had given me. I couldn't leave without it. Panic surged through me as I ransacked my room, tossing everything on the floor in a frantic search. Books, clothes, and papers flew in every direction as I desperately searched for the precious necklace. My breathing grew rapid, and tears threatened to spill from my eyes. It felt as if the walls were closing in on me, the room shrinking with each passing second.

"Where is it? Where could it be?" I muttered to myself, my voice shaking with frustration. Memories of my grandmother's comforting presence flashed before me—her warm smile, her gentle hands, the way she would hold me close and whisper words of encouragement. I couldn't bear the thought of leaving without her blessing, her protection. Just as I was on the verge of giving up, a glimmer caught my eye. There it was, my cross necklace! "Oh, Grandma, I couldn't do this without you! Thank you for helping me find it!" I whispered, my voice choked with emotion. As if she could hear me.

I didn't care, I believed she was right there with me, spirit and all.

I took a moment to compose myself, feeling the cool metal of the necklace in my hand. The panic subsided, and I quickly secured the necklace around my neck, feeling it's comforting weight against my skin. With a deep breath, I gathered my things once more and headed out the door, leaving a note on my pillow, letting my family know my plans and how much I loved them. I knew they would never understand this.

As I ran up the road to Henry's house, I caught a glimpse of a shadowy figure. It looked like a man but dark, like a specter.

"Crazy." I thought to myself. *"Maybe I'm just seeing things."* Nonchalantly shrugging my shoulders, I continued to Henry's house, but the moment I got closer, I saw the figure again by the fence. Panic gripped me, and I began banging on Henry's door.

"Henry," I yelled. "It's Cora from up the road. Let me in! C'mon, open up!" I looked around again, and it was gone. *I must be losing my mind,* I thought to myself. I continued to bang on the door. "Henry, Henry! Open up!"

"Who in God's green earth is at my door at this hour?" I heard from inside the house. "Who's at my door?" Henry yelled.

"It's me, Cora, from up the road. Please open the door!"

"Cora? Cora Hughes?" What are you doing at my house at this hour?" Henry replied.

"Henry, we just found out my Uncle Arthur passed away in London. Please open the door."

"I'm coming," Henry said.

As I stood helpless outside, not knowing what I just saw, it was refreshing to see Henry open the door.

"Henry, I'm sorry to bother you at this hour. I decided to get on a ship heading out for London this morning. I can't go by myself; you know how they are with single women trying to get on a ship alone. Can you please go with me? I just have to say goodbye to my uncle Arthur. You know how much I loved him."

I really didn't know what else to say. I felt a pang of guilt for lying, but I knew the truth would come out sooner or later. I would tell him eventually. Besides, it might do us both good to get out of this town.

"Cora, I don't know about that. That's at least a ten-day trip there and ten days back. I don't have anything packed. Couldn't you have your brother go with you? I have a lot going on right now."

I had to think fast. This was my one chance to get on this ship before it left.

"Henry, I don't want to go with my brother. I wanted to go with you. I know I'm a few years younger, but I always thought you were so attractive. I know now is not the right time to tell you this, but it's the only chance I have to be with you alone and get to know who you are. You're the only person I trust coming with me."

"Really Cora? Why didn't you ever say anything to me?"

"Because Henry, I knew you were grieving the loss of your wife. I just thought it was too early to tell you. If we don't leave now, I don't know when we'll have time to get to know each other without everyone always being around."

"OK, Cora," Henry said. "Let me get my things."

I was starting to feel like we'd never get on this ship. *C'mon Henry, Hurry up!* I thought as I paced back and forth in his living room. I glanced out the window one last time and didn't see anything. *Maybe my mind is going crazy,* I thought. I've definitely been thinking of "Jack the Ripper" a little too much lately.

"Henry," I yelled. "Are you ready yet? The boat will be leaving soon."

"I'm coming now," Henry said as we walked out the door.

"Thanks for coming with me, Henry. I really appreciate it."

I didn't want him to know which ship we were getting on, so I had to create a diversion. "Henry, the ship leaves in the next few minutes; we should probably run the rest of the way so we can make it. Just follow me; I know which one we're getting on."

As we got closer to the docks, the market square came alive with the hustle and bustle of everyday morning traders. The air was thick with the smell of fresh bread, and the calls of vendors echoed throughout the streets. Thankfully, there were so many people in the area that Henry had no clue he was getting on a ship to Whitechapel.

"C'mon, Henry, it's this one right here," I yelled.

Pushing through the crowd, I glanced up and saw that shadow figure again, this time heading onto our ship. A chill ran down my spine as I saw him disappear without a trace.

I couldn't tell Henry about this shadow figure I saw. If I did, he wouldn't go with me. I felt terrible for not telling the truth, but I felt as if the fate of the world was in my hands. I had to help solve these cases. And at last, I was here on the ship to Whitechapel. I pulled out my cross necklace and held it for a minute. "Grandma, I know you're here with me. I sure could use your help. Let's solve these cases together."

No sooner had I whispered these words than I heard the call for one last boarding.

"All aboard," the captain yelled. As we finally brought in our things and sat down. At last, the journey had begun.

Chapter 3
The Creature Inside the Ship

Finally, we made it. I'm not even sure how I pulled this off. There was an eerie feeling I hadn't felt before. The ship loomed in front of us like a shadowy overcast, its towering masts barely visible against the dark, moonlit sky. It was cold and dark inside the ship, and the air was thick with the smell of damp wood and something far more sinister. It smelled as if death had overcome us. My stomach churned with unease, and I wasn't quite sure if I had made the right choice by doing this. But it was a little too late to turn back now, I thought.

As we stepped inside, the shadows seemed to stretch and twist, playing tricks on my eyes. I couldn't get over seeing this shadow creature when I entered the ship. It had flickered at the edge of my vision, a fleeting glimpse of something otherworldly. Why was it following me? Why did it get on our ship?

All I knew was that it was in here with me, and I had no way to escape.

As Henry and I put our items down, I looked around again, trying to shake off the creeping sense of dread. The ship was a marvel of intricate woodwork and ornate carvings, every surface adorned with symbols and inscriptions. A few other passengers were still settling in, their hushed voices and hurried movements adding to the tense atmosphere.

"Henry, I whispered. Does this ship seem different to you? It feels authentic and quite unique from any other ship I've been on. Look here. Have you ever seen so much detail and wording inscribed in so many places? What language is this?"

Henry examined the carvings with a furrowed brow, "Cora, you are correct. The patterns on the edge of these tables seem to repeat themselves. I have never been on anything quite like it."

"Wait a minute," I said, a memory surfacing from the depths of my mind.

"I've seen this language a long time ago." The inscription says, "Bellator Lucis." I remembered my grandmother mentioning this phrase when I was younger. I couldn't for the life of me remember what it was about.

It's so beautiful, I thought to myself. I tried to remember the other wording but it eluded me, like a dream slipping away upon waking. It almost felt like I had been here before. At a different time, for a different purpose.

Just as that thought crossed my mind, I looked up and the shadow creature was peering through the door at the end of the hall. It was tall and gaunt, its form barely discernible in the dim light. The creature's skin was an ashen gray, blending smoothly with the darkness around. Its eyes were two hollow voids, absorbing all light and emitting an eerie, unsettling glow. Wisps of shadow seemed to emanate from its body, like smoke curling from a dying fire, giving it an otherworldly, almost ethereal appearance. Long, bony fingers clutched the doorframe, and I could see the faint outline of sharp claws that looked capable of tearing through flesh with ease. The creature's presence radiated a cold, malevolent energy that sent chills down my spine. I felt fear grip me, freezing me in place as I locked eyes with the creature, its gaze seeming to pierce through to my very soul.

I looked over to tell Henry what I had just seen, but Henry was gone! "Henry," I yelled, panic rising in my chest. "Where are you?"

My heart started beating faster as I couldn't find Henry anywhere. Something told me to pull out the necklace that my grandmother had given me. I reached for the necklace underneath my clothing, and it started to radiate a light that I had never seen before. The glow was warm and comforting, contrasting sharply with the cold, oppressive atmosphere of the ship. Drawn inexplicably towards the door, I slowly started walking down the hallway. I had no idea why I was walking closer to this creature I saw. As I came closer to the door, I gently started to push it open. Just as the door started to move, I heard Henry yell down the hallway. "Cora, get away from the door! What ship do you have us on?" I heard Henry yell.

"Henry, is that really important right now?" I yelled as I ran towards him down the hallway, my breath coming in short gasps.

"Cora, did you get us on the ship going to Whitechapel, London?"

I didn't know what to say as I was completely out of breath from running. I looked back, and the shadow creature was gone again. Henry was at the other end of the hallway waiting for me.

"Cora, are we on the ship going to Whitechapel, London?" He said again.

"Henry, I don't know what's going on, okay? I just wanted to help the people of Whitechapel. I know I can catch this "Jack the Ripper" guy. Henry, I had to do something. I'm sorry I lied to you."

"Cora, you have no idea what you've done."

"I don't understand what you mean, Henry?"

As I said this, the creature came from behind Henry and walked with him towards me.

"Henry," I yelled. "Watch out!"

"Like I said, Cora, you have no idea what you've done."

Henry's eyes started to turn red and the closer he got, his teeth started to change. I started running for my life! Racing through the ship, I thought I had gotten away from

Henry. But just as I had finally caught my breath, I looked up and he was standing in front of me.

"Cora, we need to talk," Henry said, his voice eerily calm.

I had nowhere to run. It was over. I was going to die, and I didn't even have a chance to make it to Whitechapel. Crying and full of fear, Henry pulled me by the arm and took me into a secluded room.

"Stop crying," Henry said. You have no reason to fear me or the creature. We've been watching over you since you've been born. I knew you were going to come search for me one day. I knew your plans all along."

"Wait, what?" I said to Henry, confusion mingling with my fear. "I don't understand what you mean?"

"Cora, you aren't aware of who you are or what you are. You are our last hope."

"What do you mean?" I asked, my voice trembling. "I don't understand any of this."

"Cora, my name is Henry, but I'm not human. I'm part of a Vampire Clan, also known as the "Bellator Lucis Clan." We have been protecting humans for thousands of years until now. Our rival vampires "The Invictus Clan" attacked us without warning or notice. They have killed all the

"Consilium" of our Clan. The other vampires have either died by their hands or are serving as slaves to them. We were guided to you by the Divine as our last hope. You will save the human race. But we will show you how to use your powers while we are on our way to Whitechapel."

I didn't know how to respond. My mind was reeling, spinning with confusion and disbelief. I felt as though the floor had dropped out from under me, leaving me in a freefall of emotions. I sat there, frozen, my breath coming in shallow, rapid bursts as I tried to process everything Henry had just said. It felt like my world had been turned upside down in an instant. A vampire clan? A prophecy? Powers within me? It was too much to comprehend. I could hear my heart pounding in my ears, each beat echoing the rising tide of panic inside me. My hands started to tremble and I clenched them into fists to try and steady myself. I needed to ground myself, to find some semblance of normalcy in this sea of madness. Taking a deep breath, I closed my eyes and tried to think clearly.

"Henry, this is a lot to deal with right now. All I wanted to do was solve the murders for "Jack the Ripper." Now you're telling me I'm the savior of the world? Is that correct?" The room around me seemed to fade into the background as I grappled with my thoughts. I was just a girl from Massachusetts with dreams of solving crimes and making a difference. How could I possibly be the savior of the world? The weight of that responsibility felt crushing, an impossible burden that I was utterly unprepared to bear.

"Yes, that is correct," Henry said.

Henry's words echoed in my mind; I needed a drink after hearing this. I opened my eyes to look at him, searching for some hint that this was all a joke or a mistake. But his expression was earnest. This was real. This was happening. And somehow, I was at the center of it all. But honestly, how could I save the entire world? Their entire Vampire Clan was defeated, and they expected me to save them. I solve crimes and research things. I'm no fighter. How in the world is any of this possible?

"Henry, I'm not a fighter." I finally said out loud. I'm just someone who researches and solves mysteries. No one would even notice if I'm gone. How could I possibly save the world?"

"Cora, you are whom the Divine has chosen. We will show you the powers that are within you and how to use them. But you must trust that the Divine exists and will protect you."

Well, what choice did I really have? I thought to myself. It was either this, die, or go back to Massachusetts. None of these options were what I really wanted, especially the dying one. I could already see the headlines: "Teen Prodigy Turns World Savior – Or Vampire Snack."

I took a deep breath in and allowed my thoughts to ponder on this insane ideology that I'm now a part of, "Give me a moment, Henry." I said, trying to sound as though this was a perfectly ordinary request and not the craziest moment of my life.

After standing there for a few minutes pacing the floor and trying to comprehend everything, I knew I had to give Henry a response. "OK, Henry, I'll help you. If I die, it might as well be to help save the world."

"Good," Henry said. We'll begin training tomorrow."

I didn't know what I had gotten myself into. I wish I had someone to talk to. Someone who could hear me and maybe offer a shred of sanity in this whirlwind. As these thoughts swirled in my mind, my necklace started to light up again. I didn't know what was going on, but I was too tired to care at this point. I just wanted to rest.

"Henry, can you show me to my room?" I asked. "Of course, Cora." As he led me down the hall, the ship's wooden floor creaked beneath our feet until we reached a small, cozy room.

I stepped inside and looked around. The room was simple, with a small bed, a wooden chair, and a tiny porthole that offered a view of the moonlit sea. It was nothing like home, but it would do. I felt a lump form in my throat, but I was too drained to even cry. As my head hit the pillow, I drifted off to sleep.

Chapter 4
Training Begins

Last night was a whirlwind, a series of strange events I couldn't quite wrap my head around. As I stirred awake, my eyes fixed on the windows, the events of the previous night replayed in my mind like a fragmented story. Had I really seen Henry turn into a vampire? The idea seemed absurd, yet the memory felt vivid. Where is Henry anyway? The last thing I remember was something about training that needed to take place so I could save the world. I chuckled inwardly at the thought, feeling a touch of disbelief. *I must be losing it,* I thought.

"If only grandma could be here now, she may get a good laugh," I said under my breath.

Almost as if she could hear me, my necklace started to radiate light, filling the room with a soft glow. I grabbed it with my hand and said, "Grandma, what do you need me to know?"

I whispered, hoping for an answer, but before I could get an answer, I heard a loud bang on the door.

"Cora, it's time to wake up. We have a lot of work to do."

"That sounds great, Henry, but unfortunately, the clothes I brought with me weren't made to "train" in," I yelled back in sarcasm.

Henry's response was quick, "Here," Henry said, tossing some clothes on the bedroom floor. "Hurry up, we need to get going."

I hurried up, and threw on the clothes, and met him in the hallway. The dim light cast shadows on his face, making his eyes look even more intense.

"You're not gonna turn into a vampire on me again, are you Henry?" I asked half-joking.

"Actually, that's exactly what I'm going to do," he replied, "Cora, do you remember when you saw the word, "Bellator Lucis?""

"Yes, I remember."

"Can you recall the meaning of that word?"

"No, I can't. But I remember seeing it before; I just don't remember where."

"The word 'Bellator Lucis' is Latin. It means 'Warrior of Light'. For centuries, we have been able to keep peace between humans and vampires. We mainly prey on animals and use their blood to survive. The other clan of vampires is called "The Invictus Clan." We were all at peace until a vampire named Austrodomus decided that we should be like Gods over humans, not protecting them.

He rallied up a group of some of the most powerful vampires on Earth. Nothing could stop them. The name "Invictus" means undefeatable. They knew in order to rule over the humans and The Bellator Lucis clan; they would need to take out the council and gain all the powers of each ancient member. With nowhere to turn to, most of our clan either died or became slaves. We were led by the Divine powers of the universe to you as our last hope."

The weight of his words settled on me like a heavy rock. I could feel the gravity of the situation, but there was no time for hesitation.

"So, what's next?" I asked, hiding my nervousness, trying to sound more confident than I felt.

"We will now begin your training. The first thing you need to do is lift your hands to the sky and repeat these words three times. OK? Are you ready, Cora?"

I was still trying to play catch up on what Henry just told me. I didn't really have much time to think about anything.

"Yes, Henry. What do I need to repeat?"

"Take a deep breath before you repeat this phrase each time. You will repeat these words.

'Aperta ad vires universi' This means, "I am open to receiving the powers of the Universe.""

I lifted my hands to the sky, cleared my head, and became calm. I took a deep breath in, lifted my head, and said:

"Aperta ad vires universi"

"Aperta ad vires universi"

"Aperta ad vires universi"

The room suddenly fell silent before a fierce wind howled through the windows, engulfing me in its raw energy. I began to see everything in and around me and through walls. I could hear mice chewing and conversations of others on the ship. My necklace glowed brighter than ever, and I felt power beyond anything I could ever imagine. I felt invincible.

"Now fight me," Henry commanded.

"As you wish," I replied.

Henry moved first, his fists a blur as he lunged towards me. I sidestepped effortlessly, feeling every muscle and sinew in my body with perfect precision. He spun, aiming a high kick at my head, but I ducked and countered with a swift punch to his ribs. He staggered back, eyes wide with surprise.

"You are fast," he grunted, rubbing his side.

"What is even happening?" I said, a little confused.

He came at me again; this time, his demeanor changed, and rage increased with each punch. I dodged each and every movement and was in and out faster than the bullet shooting from my grandfather's revolver. Our interactions were both deadly and powerful. The room seemed to blur around us, our focus solely on each other. Henry started to change. His eyes were red with furry, and his teeth were sharp like that of a knife cutting into flesh. He was angry. He saw the power of the Divine and couldn't touch it. His powers were weak compared to mine.

I saw an opening and took it, delivering a powerful kick to his chest.

"Oh my God!" I yelped as Henry flew back and hit the floor. He pushed himself up, his eyes glinting with anger and frustration.

Henry was doing all he could to stop me, but he couldn't touch me. I was too powerful, too strong. I was complete. For the first time in my life, I knew who I was. My name was Cora Hughes, but I was the Divine!

"Now Cora, fight the Shadow Man," Henry yelled.

A dark figure emerged, its presence sinister and threatening. Shadow Man was no match for my powers. I saw every direction he was going in. His stare would have normally frightened me just to look at him. But now, he was afraid of me.

"Grandma," I yelled. "Show him our powers."

Not knowing how I knew she was with me, my necklace lit up, and a blue orb grew around the shadow figure. It engulfed him with no escape. He struggled, but his efforts went in vain: "Stay still, Shadow Man. She will kill you if I tell her to."

Henry started clapping his hands despite being angry from the fight.

"Well done, Cora. You have incorporated the powers of the Divine into one with yourself. I see your grandmother watches over and protects you. For the rest of the trip, you will be trained each day. I will teach you different scenarios that might come up. You will come to know the true power that you have."

I, Cora, now knew my true purpose and what I was called to do. Only a couple of days of training and we would offboard. I had never been more ready in all my life. It was time to bring justice to this world and restore balance.

The next few days were a blur of intense training. While training today, I was shown to use garlic and basically anything to stab the Invictus vampires in the heart. Now, I also needed to learn the powers of the Ancient "Bellator Lucis" clan. Each Ancient member had certain powers.

"Cora," Henry said. "We had 6 Ancient members on our counsel. Each of them had a power. You will learn the powers and use them to defeat the Invictus Clan. The first ancient member, named Atticus, used elements of Earth, Wind, and Water to protect the humans. If any vampire even tried to come close to the humans, they would use the elements to keep the enemies at bay.

The second ancient member was Simon; he used the power of thought to confuse his enemies. All vampires can hear thoughts. So, when his enemies would come to attack, Simon would twist the thoughts of those around the vampires and drive them crazy.

The third ancient member was named Draco. His name to us was Dracula. But by the name Draco, his armies were formed. He carried the power of war. The anger in his heart was enough to drive a civilization to destruction.

The fourth member was Cassius. She held the power of becoming invisible to her enemies. If she ever felt danger coming, she could disappear in plain sight.

The fifth member, named Kyros, was known for his ability to outwit his opponents and make them believe in something that didn't exist. And last but not least, the final member of the Ancient clan was named Zion. He was the most powerful of all the ancient counsel. He held the power to change time. This was important, especially in war. If at any point we were losing in battle, he could turn back the time to change the outcome.

"We are still not sure how the Invictus Clan was able to get past all of our council members. From what we have heard, Austrodomus was very close to our Ancient members. He befriended them and came to be the closest ally they had. To get past all of these powers, he must have studied them very closely and caught all of them off guard. It was brilliant for them but a huge loss for us. He must have learned when they would be at their weakest.

With all that said, let's begin our training."

"You must start each training session with a clear mind. You must learn how to do this without instruction. Your grandmother will help you along this journey. She will guide you through the process. Touch your necklace, and let's begin.

The first thing I want you to do is stand at the edge of this ship. Call upon the waters of the sea and the wind in the sky. Create a storm in front of our ship." Henry instructed.

I took a deep breath and tried to command the elements. It sounded pretty easy. Just go to the edge of the ship and create a storm. It should be no problem.

"Wind in the sky and water of the sea create a storm in front of our ship," I yelled, but nothing happened. OK, I thought. Let me try again.

"Wind in the sky and water of the sea create a storm in front of our ship."

Again, nothing.

"Henry," I yelled. "This isn't working. What am I doing wrong?"

Henry's voice was calm but firm, "Cora, you need to clear your mind and listen to the Divine. By doing so, you will see the power of the universe."

OK, I thought, let's give this one last try. I took a deep breath in and slowly released it. I calmed my heart and my mind.

"Grandma," I said. "Help me," I whispered.

I looked to the sky, raised my hands, and said, "Wind in the sky, and water of the sea. Create a storm in front of our ship."

My necklace glowed, and suddenly, the wind howled, and the sea churned violently. The waves of the sea started fiercely crashing into each other.

"How's this, Henry? Good enough for you?" I asked, a triumphant smile spreading across my face.

"Well done, Cora. You're a fast learner."

Breathing heavily, I stood tall, my heart racing with exhilaration. For the first time, I felt truly unstoppable.

"The next few training sessions will need to be mind and energy-focused," Henry said, pacing in front of me. "Since most of our counsel could control thoughts, feelings, and rage. It is important to learn not only how to feel these emotions but distinguish each emotion to perfection."

"Now, Cora, tell me. Have you ever tried to confuse anyone? Besides me getting on this ship?" Henry asked, his gaze piercing.

I smirked, "Well, Henry, I would say that was my best scheme yet. But, to answer your question, yes."

"Then calm your mind and confuse the Shadow Man," Henry said.

I laughed, feeling a surge of mischief, and said, "Oh, Shadow Man, you're in for a treat." But what shall I do to confuse you?"

I closed my eyes, taking a deep breath to calm my heart and mind. I had to think for a few minutes. Grandma, I thought. Let's confuse the Shadow Man, make him think he's a vampire, and have him try to bite Henry.

"Shall we begin Shadow Man?"

"OK, Henry, I'm ready."

"Go ahead, Cora," Henry replied.

"Shadow Man, you're a fierce vampire. Henry is trying to kill you. In order to stop him, you must bite him."

As I opened my eyes, I saw the Shadow Man's demeanor change. He turned toward Henry, a predatory gleam in his eyes. He lunged, fangs bared.

Laughing so hard, I called out, "Henry, Shadow Man thinks he's a vampire and is trying to bite you."

Henry's face paled. "Cora, stop him! That isn't funny."

I had to give it a minute to see the Shadow Man go after Henry. I had never laughed so hard in my life.

"OK," I said, finally composing myself. "Shadow Man, you are no longer a vampire, and Henry is your friend."

The Shadow Man immediately stopped, looking confused as he stepped back from Henry.

"This is too much fun, Henry. Can I do it again?"

Henry shook his head, a stern expression on his face. "Now, Cora, that is enough for now. But next, you will need to focus on anger. What makes you angry, Cora?"

I paused, thinking. "Well, I was mad about no one believing me when I caught Jonathan down the street stealing from the store."

Henry frowned. "No, Cora, what made you so angry that when you think about it, you will feel that way again? Something that deeply hurt you."

I took a deep breath; my heart saddened. "Well, I was angry when my grandmother passed away. She didn't deserve to die. I was so mad when I had to watch her leave me. She was my best friend."

"Cora, feel that anger. Now, do you see the cargo ship that's passing by us? Destroy it!"

I took a deep breath in and calmed my heart and my mind. I remembered sitting next to Grandma, not knowing how long she had left to live. I was so angry I had to let her go. Now, it was my turn to unleash my anger. My necklace started to glow, and I could feel the rage within me. I thought, if only that ship would blow up, my anger and hurt would be gone. Within seconds, the cargo ship exploded. I had never felt so much anger as I did in that moment.

"Henry, I would like to finish my next training tomorrow. That was enough for today." I said, my voice trembling.

As I walked out of the room, a tear streamed down my face. I didn't even realize that I was that angry. It took a lot of me to remember the contents of that day and the emptiness I felt when my grandmother left me. I knew I had to make her proud. I knew she was with me in spirit. What I wouldn't do to hold her again and tell her I loved her. As I thought this, my necklace started to glow again.

"I know you're here, grandma. I would just love to see you again."

With that, I walked back down the hallway to my bedroom. As I lay there thinking about the day I just had, I couldn't help but remember something Henry said. He told me that Austrodomus was close to the Ancient members. He said his idea was brilliant. But why did Henry say this? It was a simple reply, I suppose, but it didn't make much sense. Was Henry somehow involved in all this? And if so, why would he be training me? It just didn't add up. I'm going to keep an eye on him and keep my guard up. I couldn't show Henry any of my weaknesses.

As I tossed and turned in my bed, I finally gave way to sleep. The next morning came quickly, bringing with it my final day of training.

"Cora, are you awake?" Henry yelled, banging on the door.

"Yes, I'm awake."

"Come down to the basement of the ship," Henry called out. "Our training is down there today."

"On my way, Henry."

As I walked down to the darkest place on the ship, fear started to come over me. The narrow staircase spiraled into darkness, the flickering light of my torch casting eerie shadows on the damp, wooden walls. The air was thick and musty, carrying the scent of seaweed and old wood, mingling with the faint smell of gloom and death.

My footsteps echoed loudly in the confined space, a stark contrast to the oppressive silence that seemed to envelop everything. The creaking of the ship's hull was the only other sound, like the groans of a slumbering beast. As I reached the bottom, the dim light barely penetrated the gloom, revealing only vague shapes and outlines. The cold air down here felt different like it was pressing in on me from all sides.

A shiver ran down my spine, and I couldn't shake the feeling of unease that had settled over me.

Why did Henry want to train down here today? Something just didn't seem right. This place was far removed from the open deck where we usually trained, filled with fresh air and sunlight. Down here, it felt like we were stepping into another world, one that was darker and more dangerous.

"Cora, we're over here," Henry said.

I looked around, but I only saw Henry.

"Henry, where is the Shadow Man? Is he not training with us today?"

"He will be here shortly", Henry said.

But wait, Henry just said, "We're over here". Something is definitely wrong, I thought.

"Cora, today you will learn how to be invisible and how to change time. Are you ready?"

"Yes, Henry, I am ready."

Close your eyes and begin to picture yourself in a different place. Where do you wish to be?"

Anywhere but here would be a great start, I thought. But truthfully, I kind of wanted to be at home. For the first time in my life, I was starting to miss it.

"Have you thought of a place, Cora?"

"Yes," I replied.

"Where would you wish to go," Henry said.

I had to throw him off. I didn't want to show him my weaknesses, especially since he was acting kind of weird.

"I'd like to go to Whitechapel to see what it is like before I arrive," I replied.

"As you wish, Cora."

Close your eyes and see Whitechapel, London.

"How do I do that if I've never seen it, Henry?"

"You haven't, Cora, but the Divine has. Keep calm and think, "I want to be in Whitechapel, London.""

With that being said, I thought of being in Whitechapel the very next day. I wanted to think of a specific time as well. So, I thought about when we would offboard the ship at sunrise.

What I did was nothing more than a miracle!

I saw us getting off the ship and heading down the street. But then I noticed Henry nodding his head to someone as we got off the ship. I followed this person, remaining unseen as I envisioned it. They could only see the future me. The man that Henry nodded to gathered what looked to be the most powerful vampires. The ones Henry had spoken of.

But why was Henry trying to kill me? What was in it for him? I couldn't see much after that. I asked my grandmother to help me change time to the future. I had to know what would happen without Henry knowing what I saw. She then revealed herself to me and said, "Cora, you must not say anything about what I'm going to show you. Henry can't know this as he will die for being a traitor to the Divine."

I nodded my head, and Grandma took me by the hand. "Do you see beyond that ship over there?" my grandmother said.

"Yes," I replied.

"Look closely."

As I started to look a little closer, there was an army of God-like Creatures I hadn't seen before.

"Grandma, what are those creatures you're showing me?"

"They are a gift from the Divine. Nothing will harm you. Go now and tell no one. Henry can't know any of this."

As I came back, Henry asked me how it went.

"Henry, I think I saw that "Jack the Ripper" person everyone speaks of. I was scared to death. Is he a vampire?"

"Not that I'm aware of Cora. Did you want to learn how to change time now?"

"Yes, I'd love to!"

I had to act somewhat normal, knowing what tomorrow would bring.

"OK, here's the secret to that. You just close your eyes and think of it being daytime or night time and a place you wish to be. Then focus really hard."

"OK, let me try," I said.

I had to pretend I didn't already do this.

"I think I'll go to the store where Jonathan stole those items. I'm curious what he took anyway. I could only see him putting things in his pocket."

I closed my eyes and pictured the day and time I saw Jonathan. *What did he take,* I thought? I had to get a closer look.

As I got a little closer, I saw Jonathan taking food and putting it in his clothing. I followed him from the store to where he was going. He went home. When he went inside, I saw him pull out the items and set them on the table and then tears streamed down his face. He didn't have any money to feed his family. I felt so terrible for trying to get him in trouble. Of course, I wanted to do what was right, but now I felt awful. Not wanting to relive it anymore, I decided it was time to come back.

"OK, Henry, I know how to do it now."

I explained to him what I saw with Jonathan. He didn't suspect a thing. After the practice, I asked about the Shadow

Man again. Henry just shook his head and said, "I'm not sure where he went. I told him to be here for our practice. He has to be around here somewhere."

"OK, Henry," I replied. "I'm going to go walk around for a while and enjoy the last part of the trip before we offboard tomorrow."

As I left the room, I walked around to see if I could find the Shadow Man. But I couldn't find him anywhere. "Grandma," I said, underneath my breath. "Please protect me as we put an end to this war."

My necklace started glowing again, a warm and comforting light that reassured me she had heard my silent plea. I took a deep breath, letting the sense of calm wash over me, and made my way back to my room. The creaking of the wooden floorboard beneath my feet and the distant murmur of the ocean were the only sounds accompanying me. I knew it was up to me, and the fate of the world was in my hands. I wasn't afraid now. I saw what my grandmother showed me. I wasn't alone. I had an army behind me. One that the Invictus Clan couldn't see or expect.

Chapter 5
The Beginning of The War

This last night went by a little too quickly, leaving me with a sense of urgency mixed with anticipation, but I was ready to begin my journey.

As dawn approached, the ship's two horns blared twice, a signal that we were nearing the port. The sound echoed through the vessel, stirring a mix of excitement and apprehension within me. Despite the looming uncertainty, I couldn't shake the eerie disappearance of Shadow Man. Suspicion gnawed at me; I had begun to like him. Yes, he was scary and frightening to most, but he actually started to grow on me. The fact that he was missing had me more intrigued than ever.

I needed to search the ship one more time to see if I could find him. I had to do it without Henry noticing. As if on cue, a loud bang rattled my door.

"Cora, get up and get around. We're about to port."

"Yes, Henry, I'm aware. I heard the horns. I'll meet you at the exit as soon as we get there. I have to pack my things and get around before we get off the ship."

"OK, Cora, make sure to remember all that I taught you. I'll see you when we offboard."

The urgency in his voice spurred me into action. This was my last chance to find Shadow Man. I waited a few minutes, listening intently for any sign of Henry outside. When the coast was clear, I slipped out of my room and hurried down the hallway, trying to remember the last place I had seen him. That's when I remembered the training room. I had to hurry and get there before we got off the ship. I was running as fast as I possibly could. When I finally got to the door, I slowly pushed it open and peered inside. The room was dimly lit, shadows dancing in the corners. I tiptoed, analyzing the room for any sign of Shadow Man. I couldn't find him anywhere.

"Shadow Man," I quietly called out. Are you here? It's Cora. I'm trying to help you."

There was no response. Disappointment and frustration welled up inside me. I waited a few seconds more, with hope still brewing inside, but there was still no reply. As I started to leave, I heard footsteps approaching. Henry's voice floated down the hall, muttering to himself. I hurried up and slipped underneath the desk inside the room as fast as I could.

As I sat there quietly, trying not to make a sound, I heard Henry call out to the Shadow Man.

"Shadow Man," he called out, his voice dripping with menace. He walked closer to where I was, and his footsteps kept getting louder. I heard the faint click of a button, and a secret door opened.

"Ah, Shadow Man, there you are," Henry said, a sinister smile in his voice.

"You almost ruined it for me. I know Cora is part of the Divine, but if I didn't know any better, I would've thought you actually started liking her."

As Henry started walking away from the desk, I glanced out from underneath it to see where the Shadow Man was. He had him inside a small dark room locked inside a cage. Anger and betrayal surged through me.

"Now, Shadow Man, I hate to leave you in here like this, but I can't have you interfering with everything. We've waited too many years to have you ruin our plans for us. Once Cora Hughes is dead, we'll consider setting you free."

Henry's words cut through me like a knife. Seeing it in a vision was one thing; hearing it from his own mouth was another.

With that, Henry walked back over to the desk, pushed the button again, and left.

I couldn't believe Henry wanted me dead, I thought. I couldn't focus on that now. I had to hurry and save the Shadow Man before Henry got back. As Henry left the room, I scrambled out from under the desk and pushed the button, opening the secret door again. I rushed to the Shadow Man's cage.

"Don't worry, Shadow Man. I will save you."

He looked surprised that I came back for him. He reached out and touched my hand through the bars.

"Shadow Man, where are the keys?" I asked urgently.

He pointed to a hook near the door. I hurried over, grabbed the keys, and unlocked the cage. Shadow Man slowly stepped out, stretching his limbs cautiously.

"Shadow Man, I need you to stay close to me, but don't let Henry see you. When we off board, Henry has the strongest vampires near the ship. They are waiting to kill me. I need you to run towards the furthest ship on your right when we get off. There, you will be safe."

I couldn't reveal everything. Grandma had warned me in the vision not to trust anyone. That included Shadow Man.

He nodded, understanding the gravity of our situation. I rushed back to my room, packed my things, and headed to the exit. On our way off board, I saw Henry through the crowd. With a smirked grin, he looked at me, just as I had seen in the vision.

"Are you ready for Whitechapel, Cora?" Henry asked, his eyes scanning me suspiciously.

"Yes, I am Henry. This has been a long trip. I'm looking forward to ending this war."

With that, they started letting people offboard the ship to Whitechapel. As we were heading off the ship, hundreds of people were trying to leave. The moment was tense as people began disembarking the ship in a chaotic rush. The air was thick with fear and uncertainty.

"Why on earth would you come here?" I heard people scream.

"Do you know where you are?"

As we moved with the crowd, I glanced back, trying to spot the Shadow Man. I quickly saw his head disappear among the throng. Turning back, I noticed Henry's subtle nod. Again, just like in my vision. I had to get prepared. What was about to happen next would be the beginning of the war.

"Grandma, I love you," I said, touching my necklace. "Be with me as we end this war and bring justice back to mankind."

With that, I stepped into the foggy streets of Whitechapel.

Chapter 6
No One Leaves
Whitechapel

As the fog began to clear, the streets revealed the truth to the stories that were told. Loud screams echoed in every corner of the city. There was a nauseated feeling that came over me, and the smell of drunkenness and death seemed to linger in the air. Before me, the truth of Whitechapel was revealed. A chill ran down my spine as the city was covered in darkness and gloom. It was time. War was before me, and I was ready. Touching my necklace, I called on the Divine for insight. The cool metal seemed to pulse with energy under my fingers. I closed my eyes, quieting my mind and listening intently as I focused on the path set before me. The air was thick with tension, and every sound seemed amplified in the stillness of dawn.

I overheard two vampires talking in hushed tones, their voices dripping with anticipation.

"Which power do you think she will use when she realizes who we are?" One of them asked.

"We must be prepared for all of them," the other vampire said.

As I lifted my head, I could see where they stood. I had to act quickly and decisively. Let me confuse their minds, I thought.

Gathering my courage, I shouted, "Vampires of the Invictus Clan, your enemies are next to you. They are not your friends. "Destroy them, I command you!"

The vampires turned on each other, chaos erupting as they tore into one another. Blood and snarls filled the air. Henry, noticing the commotion, started running towards them.

"Henry, where are you going?" I yelled.

"Cora, stay back. I'm going to see what's going on." He shouted over his shoulder.

Henry disappeared into the shadows. I knew it was my chance to escape and make a plan. In my vision, my grandmother showed me these invisible creatures that only I could see. They were part of the Divine, sent here to protect me.

I rushed over to the very last ship, where I sent the Shadow Man. Looking around, I could see no one.

This couldn't be right, I thought to myself. "Grandma, what's going on?" I whispered, clutching my necklace. It started to glow a soft blue and angled downward on the street as if to guide me. I followed the light through a dark alley, the oppressive silence pressing in on me. The light led me to a nondescript door. I grabbed the handle and pushed it open. When I walked inside, the door shut behind me with a finality that made my heart pound.

I followed the light to the top of the steps, guiding me to a room filled with an ethereal glow. Voices murmured from within. As I approached, I heard a voice that sounded like my grandmother.

"Come inside, Cora," she said. We're all in here waiting for you."

I felt relieved that someone knew who I was. That I wasn't completely alone.

"Grandma, is that you?" I called out.

"Yes, Cora, it is your grandmother. I have been watching over you for some time now."

"But grandma, why are we in the most dangerous part of Whitechapel?"

"The Invictus Clan tries to stay away from these parts." She replied. "Many down in this area have nothing to live for. They know who the vampires are, and they are not afraid to kill them."

"Grandma, did you get a chance to meet the Shadow Man?"

"Why yes, I did. He's right here."

Shadow Man stepped out from the darkness, his form slowly materializing like a wisp of smoke solidifying into flesh. His presence was both comforting and eerie, a blend of shadow and substance that defied the natural order. His eyes, deep pools of midnight, held a wisdom and sadness that spoke of centuries lived in the margins of light and dark.

"Shadow Man, I'm so glad to see you!" I exclaimed, my voice breaking the spell of silence that had enveloped us. His nod was slight, but the understanding in his eyes spoke volumes. In that moment, the fear that had gripped my heart loosened its hold. We were not alone in this fight, and his presence reaffirmed that the Divine's protection was tangible, not just a figment of desperate hope.

Grandmother began, and we all started discussing how we could put an end to this war.

But our time was cut short by loud screams from the street. The sounds grew closer, sending chills down my spine.

"Cora, follow the light." My grandmother urged.

Then, she was gone.

I looked all around for her. "Grandma, Grandma, where are you?" I yelled, panic rising.

I started to head down the stairs and heard screams, getting closer to the door. I needed to leave, but how?

Then I remembered my training, calming my mind and heart. I took a deep breath. "I am now invisible," I whispered under my breath.

The door burst open, and a horde of vampires stormed in, their eyes glowing with predatory intent. They moved swiftly; their fangs bared, but they couldn't see me. I remained invisible. The Shadow Man, true to his nature, melded smoothly into the shadows, becoming one with the darkness. The invisible creatures that guarded us circled silently; their presence felt but unseen.

"Ah!" I heard one of them yell. "She has to be here. Go find her before she gets away!"

The vampires searched frantically, overturning tables and tearing through the room in their hunt. Their frustration grew as they found nothing, their growls echoing through the small space. I watched them, my heart pounding in my chest, but I remained unseen and undetected. As they were heading to leave, I noticed there were stakes to stab them with lying on the table. An idea sparked in my mind. I nodded to the invisible creatures, signaling them. We each grabbed a stake and, moving with silent precision, drove the sharpened wood into the vampires' hearts. Within seconds, they perished and turned into gray bodies. As I became visible again, I started to walk out the door when I noticed one of the vampires had a marking on his wrist of ancient times. I walked over to the body to see what the marking said.

Was this an ancient member I just killed?

Intrigued, I knelt to examine it more closely. The inscription was in Latin, reading, "Mors me tangere non potest "—"Death cannot touch me."

As I threw his wrist down to leave, the ashes began to coalesce, reforming the body I had just seen perish. Panic surged through me as the vampire's body reanimated. I knew this power was of the ancient members.

I calmed my mind and my heart and called upon the Divine and my grandmother. My body started to radiate pure light, filling the room with a blinding brilliance. The vampire, now fully revived, recoiled at the sight of my radiant form.

"Vampire," I said, my voice steady and filled with authority. "You should've stayed down. Now, you will see the power of the Divine, as you have brought disgrace to the ancient members. It is the Divine that executes judgment."

With that being said, the vampire started to rush towards me. My body floated above the ground, glowing with an intense, otherworldly light. I grabbed the vampire by the neck, and as my hands made contact, I could feel the life force being drawn from him. He struggled, his eyes wide with fear and rage, but he was powerless against the might of the Divine. His body ignited, flames consuming him until nothing remained but a pile of ashes.

"Let us go now," I commanded. "Before it's too late and the ships leave with the vampires on them. They cannot leave this town."

With that said, we left the building. The city was in complete chaos. Many were drunk alcoholics living on the streets. Others were prostitutes trying to make a living in the town. Never had I seen a more disastrous place. Henry was nowhere to be found.

We cut all the ties to the ships that were at the docks. The Divine creatures pushed them off into the sea, crushing them as they got further out. Smoke from the fire swirled in the wind, and pieces of crushed wood from the ships floated against the tide. The smell of death lingered in the air. We couldn't let any escape. Shadow Man slipped in and out of the darkness, snatching the vampires one by one. I picked up a sword that one of the vampires held. Its inscription read, "mortem finalem" or the "final death". Gripping the sword, I felt its power. The silver shined off the firelit sky. The handle attached itself to me as if to become one with its vigor as they rushed in from all angles. I began slashing each one, using the sword of death and piercing their hearts. Blood splattered as screams echoed throughout the night. The fire from the battle now engulfed the town, and chaos was everywhere.

Amid the array of commotion, a silence began to sweep over the city like a curse. The smoke cleared, and the fallen vampires were only ashes against the ground as smoke from their bodies drifted in the wind. We walked throughout the city, waiting for another to appear, but they were gone. The wood creaked beneath our feet as houses continued to collapse from the fire. We knew there would be more and that the battle wasn't over. As I cleaned the blood from my sword, a flash of blue light shined against its silver edges. I took a closer look, my reflection radiating back to me. My eyes glowed with blue light, and my body was surrounded by a white hue that radiated the night sky. Shadow Man emerged next to me, his intent gaze letting me know the battle was over. We called forth the Divine creatures to help us search for any other vampires, but none had been found.

We decided it was time to settle in for the night. The Divine creatures found a small decrepit hotel untouched by the battle. Shadow Man was on the lookout now, his eyes ever watchful for any threats. He would signal us if anything came our way. Exhausted, I tossed and turned, the weight of the day heavy on my mind, hoping to close my eyes, and then I finally did.

Once asleep, I dreamt of walking through the woods to a castle. It was dark and dreary as gloom and death seemed to linger in the air. The clouds overshadowing a moonlit sky, and loud howls screamed throughout the night. There was an eerie feeling that came over me as I approached its heavy wooden doors; they creaked open, and a chilling voice greeted me.

"Come inside," I heard.

"Where am I?" I asked, cautiously stepping into the dimly lit hall.

As I said these words, a vampire appeared before my eyes.

"I am Dracula," he replied. "I have come to visit you while you sleep." The Invictus Clan took my powers as the ancient one. Here is how you can gain it back."

Tomorrow, as you awake, you will be led to a home outside the city. Vampires from the Invictus Clan will follow you to this house. In the basement, next to the stairwell, there is a crystal ball. Once you pick it up, call forth the powers of the Divine. The vampires will rush in to kill you but instead will be drawn into the crystal. Then you must throw it down and shatter it. After this, you will receive the powers they took from me."

After imparting his cryptic instructions, Dracula led me back to the door.

"You will need your strength for tomorrow. Do as I say, and you will have the power of rage to destroy the Invictus Clan."

Chapter 7
The End of the Invictus Clan

Morning came early, its light creeping into the room like an uninvited guest. The events of the previous night hung over me like a heavy shroud, but the words of Dracula resonated in my mind, a beacon guiding my path. I needed to head out now.

"Shadow Man," I called out. "Are you still here?"

I looked outside the door, only to find him sprawled on the floor, his dark form a mere shadow against the cold, hard ground.

"Shadow Man, wake up!" I shook him vigorously. "Fall asleep like that again, and I'll have Grandma put you back into the blue orb. We don't have time to waste. Follow behind me and keep an eye out. We will have the Invictus Clan following us soon, and I need your complete attention."

Groggy but alert, the Shadow Man rose, his form shifting and stretching as if awakening from a long slumber. I returned inside, grabbed my things, and headed to the door. The creatures of the Divine and Shadow Man were with me now, a silent, vigilant entourage. We headed outside the city to a white house just past the river. The path was eerily quiet, the only sound was the sound of our footsteps and the distant murmur of the water. But soon, I could hear other steps behind me, a growing cacophony of footfalls that sent a chill down my spine.

The steps started getting faster and louder. I started running as fast as I could into the house. As I rushed inside, I saw an army of vampires coming towards me. The invisible creatures sprang into action, their forms flickering as they engaged the invaders. The scene was chaotic, a whirlwind of shadows and fangs. I saw the Shadow Man run into the house and try to close the door. He couldn't hold them off.

"Shadow Man, keep the door closed as long as you can!" I shouted. "I have to go to the basement."

I dashed down the steps, my heart pounding in my chest like a war drum. Dracula's instructions echoed in my mind as I spotted the crystal ball near the stairwell at the bottom of the steps. It glimmered with an eerie light of hope and dread.

The door above splintered, and the vampires of the Invictus Clan came running into the basement after me. Their eyes gleamed with malevolent hunger; their fangs bared.

"Divine Powers," I cried out, "Return the powers of Dracula to me now!"

With that, the crystal ball began to glow, its light intensifying as it drew the vampires towards it. Their screams filled the air, growing louder and more desperate until, one by one, they were pulled into the crystal. With a final throw, I shattered it beneath my feet. Power surged through me, filling me with strength and rage.

I ran back up the steps and went outside. Bodies of the Invictus Clan littered the ground, turning to ash as the creatures of the Divine were annihilating them.

"Shadow Man," I yelled. "Get to the highest part of the house!"

We had no time to waste. I called upon the waters of the sea and the wind in the sky to kill all of the Invictus Clan that were still standing.

The sky started forming dark clouds, and the sea rose above the ground.

I closed my eyes, feeling the energy of the universe flowing through me. My feet lifted off the ground as if carried by an unseen force. As I hovered slightly above the earth, I called upon the elements, my voice a whisper in the wind. The sky began to change, dark clouds swirling and gathering with an ominous speed. They formed a churning mass above us, their dark hues contrasting sharply with the earlier morning light. A low rumble of thunder echoed across the landscape, a warning of the storm to come.

With a sudden, fierce intensity, the sea responded to my call. Waves surged higher and higher, their crests foaming and crashing with a power that matched the growing storm. The once calm river transformed into a raging torrent, the water seeming to reach for the sky.

Lightning crackled and split the heavens, jagged bolts of pure energy striking the ground with terrifying precision. Each strike found its mark, vaporizing the remaining vampires in blinding flashes of light. The air smelled of ozone, and the ground trembled with the force of the electrical onslaught.

As the lightning did its deadly work, the sea rose even higher, forming a massive wave. It loomed above the vampires, a towering wall of water that seemed to defy gravity. With a roar like a hundred hurricanes, the wave crashed down, engulfing the vampires and sweeping them away in a furious, unstoppable tide.

Once I saw all of them were dead, I called the winds and the sea off of them. I lowered myself back to the ground, my feet touching the earth lightly. The battlefield was silent now, the threat vanquished, but the memory of the storm lingered.

"Come now, Shadow Man."

"We're just getting started."

As we were leaving, I noticed a body next to one of the members of the Invictus Clan. As I got closer to it, I realized it was Henry. He was fighting alongside them to destroy us but ended up being destroyed. A wave of sadness and anger washed over me. He had made his choice, but it still hurt to see him like that. I didn't know how to react, so we just left. There was nothing I could've done to save him. Even though he would've killed me, I didn't have the heart to do the same. The Divine brought justice to Henry. That is what I kept telling myself.

We needed to leave now. There was too much work that needed to be done. We grabbed the rest of our weapons and left.

Now, Shadow Man, the creatures, and I headed throughout London, killing any members of the Invictus Clan that were left. Our final destination loomed ahead: a castle at the town's edge, home to the most powerful vampire. This was the vampire that stole the power of Zion to change time. Word quickly spread, and he knew we were coming.

The path to the castle was a confusing maze designed to mislead. We kept passing the same flower over and over, and it hit me - he was using his power to manipulate time, trapping us in a loop.

"Of course!" I thought to myself - no wonder we've been doing this for hours!

I needed to outwit him. But how I thought.

That's it! I can create an illusion to make him think we are walking the same path over and over. Then, I will enter his mind and confuse his thoughts to make him think we are part of his clan. This idea was genius.

I then closed my eyes and created an illusion of a Shadow Man and myself walking this path over and over. Then, I went into his mind.

We are part of the Invictus Clan; why do you have us walking around in circles? Let us into the castle, I thought.

A new path opened, and we followed it to the castle doors. Shadow Man, the creatures, and I were now headed into the castle. Once we got to the door, we were greeted by the top Invictus members.

"Come inside," they said.

As we entered the castle, the castle was dark with no windows and no light. The air was thick with a sense of foreboding. From the shadows, the master of the castle emerged.

The vampire holding the power of Zion now came from behind the walls.

"Welcome to the castle of the Ancient ones. I don't believe we've ever met. My name is Austrodomus.

The most powerful vampire of our kind. And what is your name?"

"My name?" I replied, a sad smile on my face. "You do not remember me, Austrodomus? Let me remind you of who I am. Thousands of years ago, we were close. The first of our kind and were created in the very image of God. We spent many lifetimes together and had many children. The love we had for each other was unbreakable. That was until you decided that power was more important than love. You decided that living forever and ruling over others was more important than even God himself. Do you remember who I am now?"

Recognition dawned in his eyes, "Eve, is that you?"

"Eve was who you knew me by then. Today, I am known as Cora Hughes. And now you're known as Austrodomus—the most powerful vampire of the Invictus Clan. You have come to shame the Divine, Austrodomus. You and I were created to protect mankind from evil, and you became the evil one. Thirsting for blood and killing the innocent. Forgetting that love is more powerful than ruling over others. The Divine has sent me to punish you for this crime. It is against God himself that you betrayed."

His gaze hardened, "No, Eve. I haven't gone against God. You have it all wrong. See, I don't believe I have sinned against him. I believe that I am him. I have been able to change time and recreate everything from start to finish. The power that I hold, I can never die. It is to me that the world should worship."

"Then you shouldn't be afraid to fight me, Austrodomus."

With those words, a brilliant light began to emanate from my body, growing in intensity until it enveloped me completely. The power within me surged like a dormant volcano finally awakening, its heat and energy coursing through my veins. I could feel the presence of the Divine forces and my grandmother, their strength and wisdom merging with mine, guiding my actions.

We moved as one through the labyrinthine halls of the castle, the walls echoing with the sounds of our battle. The stairwells were narrow and winding, each step a new challenge as vampires lunged at us from the shadows. But the Divine creatures – beings of light and purity – fought valiantly at our side, their ethereal forms cutting through the darkness. They held back our enemies, their radiant swords clashing with the claws and fangs of the undead.

The air was thick with the scent of ancient stone and the metallic tang of blood. Shadows danced wildly on the walls, cast by the flickering torches that lined the corridors. My breath came in short, determined gasps as we pressed forward, my mind focused on the task at hand.

Finally, we burst into the family room of the castle. It was a grand space filled with relics and artifacts from centuries past. The fireplace roared with a hellish flame, casting a sinister glow across the room. And there, resting against the hearth, was the sword of death – a weapon forged in the fires of creation, capable of ending life, no matter how powerful.

With a sense of destiny, I reached for the sword. Its hilt was cold and heavy in my hand, yet it felt as if it had been made for me, fitting perfectly in my grasp.

The moment I touched it, a wave of memories washed over me, ancient and profound. I remembered who I was. I was Eve—the first and the last. Loved by God, chosen to carry out His will, destined to bring Divine justice to this world and to protect the innocent from harm.

Austrodomus, the most powerful vampire of the Invictus Clan, emerged from the shadows. His eyes gleamed with a mixture of recognition and defiance.

"Eve," he hissed, his voice dripping with malice. "You think you can defeat me?"

Without hesitation, I moved forward, the sword of death leading my charge. The blade glowed with an inner light, reflecting the fire within my soul. With a single, swift motion, I drove the sword into Austrodomus's heart. His eyes widened in shock and pain as the weapon pierced his chest, the glow from the blade spreading through his body.

For a moment, everything was still. Then, I felt a spirit lift from within me—a release of ancient power that had been bound for too long. A tear streamed down my face, not just for the battle I fought and won but for the realization of my true identity and purpose.

"I am Eve," I whispered, my voice filled with both sorrow and triumph. "The first and the last. Loved by God and chosen to carry out His will. To bring Divine justice to this world and protect the innocent."

Epilogue

After Austrodomus had fallen, the rest of the Invictus Clan met their end swiftly. They had to be eradicated to ensure they would never again threaten the world. The castle echoed with their final, desperate cries before silence reclaimed its ancient halls.

Years later, the shadow over Whitechapel lifted. The streets, once feared and avoided, became lively with laughter and light.

As for me, Cora Hughes, I returned to Boston, Massachusetts. The journey home was filled with a bittersweet nostalgia. My family greeted me with open arms, their love a balm for my weary soul.

Boston might have been just a small town, but to me, it was everything. The scent of the ocean, the sound of children playing, and the vibrant colors of autumn leaves reminded me of what I had been fighting for. Though my powers remained within me, I chose to embrace a quieter existence. I wanted to be just "Cora Hughes" for now.

But in the stillness of the night, when the stars shone brightly above, I knew that if darkness threatened to rise once more, I would be ready.

THE END

www.ingramcontent.com/pod-product-compliance
Lightning Source LLC
Chambersburg PA
CBHW051547120626

46551CB00013B/1407